Tell The World It's A Girl
By Jeanmela Murray

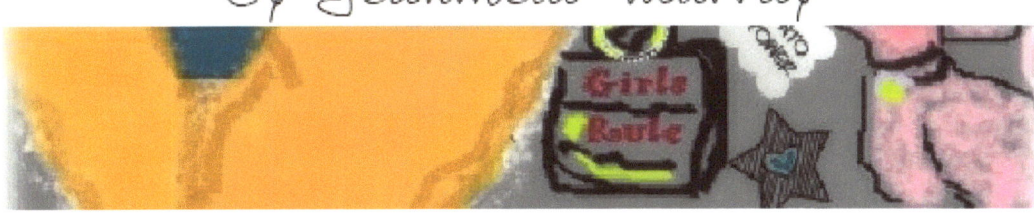

Tell The World It's A Girl.
2ⁿᵈ Edition Copyright © May 2015
By Jeanmela Murray

A Cupcake & Giggles Publishing

This title is Also brought to you by: C.A.R.E IMPRINT (Children Are Reading Everyday)

All rights reserved. No part of this publication may be reproduced, distributed, or transmitted in any form or by any means, including photocopying, recording, or other electronic or mechanical methods, without the prior written permission of the publisher, except in the case of brief quotations embodied in critical reviews and certain other non-commercial uses permitted by copyright law. For permission requests, write to the publisher, addressed "Attention: Permissions Coordinator," at the email address below.

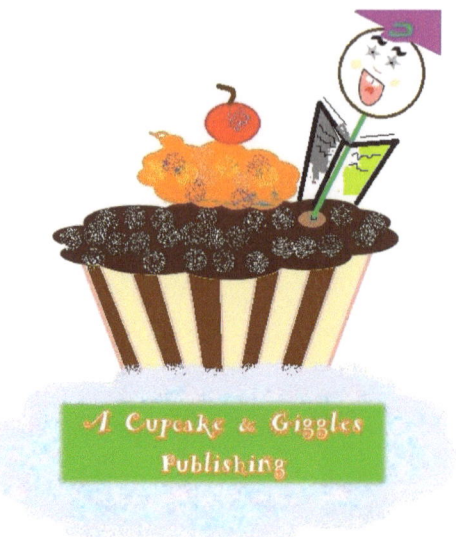

WWW.ICARE.IMPRINT@GMAIL.COM

Like us on FACEBOOK: WWW.FACEBOOK.COM/TELLTHEWORLDCHILDRENSBOOKSERIES

Also available from this author: Tell the world it's a boy

Ordering Information: Tell the world book series are available at: acupcakeandgigglespublishing.com, amazon.com, specialty bookstores and online boutiques. Please Contact a cupcake and giggles publishing for more details.
Quantity sales. Special discounts are available on quantity purchases by corporations, associations, and others. For details, contact the publisher at the email address above.

Published, Printed and Distributed in the United States of America
Printed and Distributed in Charleston, SC
ISBN-13: 978-0996384704
ISBN-10: 0996384707
BISAC: Juvenile Nonfiction / Family / New Baby
2nd Edition Paperback May 2015
Book Design/Illustration by Jeanmela Murray
Cover Model: Zoee Catelaya

●Tell The World It's A Girl●

To LOVE: Out of the darkest night the sun did rise and gave me the most incredible prize! A gift, a treasure... A Daughter!! I waited for you all my life! With you, I'm filled with all I need. You are my greatest inspiration; I get to see a brand new world through your eyes and it's refreshingly beautiful. Thank you for choosing me! Let us forever go to the moon tonight my sweet precious baby girl! I love you beyond the skies, with no end...My Cupcake, My Orchid, My Lotus Flower, My Gamble, My Sunshine, My Rebel Heart, My Little Miss Sassy, My Life, My Zoe Catelaya 🌕...

GO BE BRILLIANT!!

Love Always,

Mommy (Your endless supply of love) ∞

◇◇◇

To My Amazing Family, Friends, and Supporters

THANK YOU, THANK YOU, THANKYOU ☺ XOXO

◇◇◇

Daughters all over the world...OWN YOUR GREATNESS- Be Exceptional...No-one can put the color in your Dream but YOU!! Special Mention: Destinee, Malaya, Makaiya, Shalaya, Shayla, Aijzsa, Lataisha, Stephine, Sharelle, Paris, Denea, Essence, Raven, Aanaya, Olivia, Bella (Beautiful Angel), Yamari, Yimorah, Yanoviah, Riley, Giani, Lalah

◇◇◇

My Parents: Melvin Leathers & Mamie Cora Jean WITHOUT YOU, THERE IS NO ME or ZOEE...

I LOVE YOU!!! ∞

◇◇◇

My new Angels-Aunt Jadi <My Rainbow>: Epitome of Sass, Fierceness, Beauty, and Strength

Aunt Dot: Love, Grace, & Nurturer

My Sister Joy: Taken so soon but your light will continually shine through your niece and myself ☼ Love U

●Tell The World It's A Girl●

An Inscription to My Daughter

I AM UNSTOPPABLE

_____
NAME

_____
FROM

ISBN-13: 978-0996384704 / ISBN-10: 0996384707

●Tell The World It's A Girl●

•THANK HEAVEN FOR LITTLE GIRLS•

It's a Girl, a *Beautiful* little Girl; an Angel you are

And we are happily in love with you....

Oooh, what lovely eyes, nose, and lips

Oh my precious daughter, before you, the world seemed like a total

eclipse....

Girls are God's Gift to the World

It's a Girl, a **Mesmerizing** little Girl; what an Angel you are! A dream come true the first time we laid eyes on you....

The moment you were born,

Flowers of wonder began growing in your presence.

Oh baby, You're Perfect in every way! Hair filled with magical curlicues, skin so soft, scent so sweet, and totally kissable little feet....

● Tell The World It's A Girl ●

Don't be just a spectator of life

It's a Girl, a Heaven-Sent little Girl; what an Angel you are!

Time stood still the moment you were born....

The world is oh so busy and for the rest of our lives no nap or sleep for We,

But there is no place on Earth we'd rather be....

I AM ENOUGH

My life is important

UNO 1   DOS 2   TRES 3

QUATRO 4   CINCO 5   SEIS 6

SIETE 7   OCHO 8   NUEVE 9   DIEZ 10

●Tell The World It's A Girl●

It's a Girl, a Spirited little Girl; what an Angel you are!

Thank you for choosing us; in our hearts is where you will always be....

Blushing little jowls and giggly giggles, but

Mommy and Daddy can't help it; you're as pretty as pretty can be

You'll forever feel the fullness of our hearts;

They flutter through the sky as kisses and land on your cheek....

● Tell The World It's A Girl ●

●Tell The World It's A Girl●

It's a Girl, a Delightful little Girl; what an Angel you are!

The cure for sad faces and broken hearts morning, noon, and night....

One look at you and this unyielding world seems new....

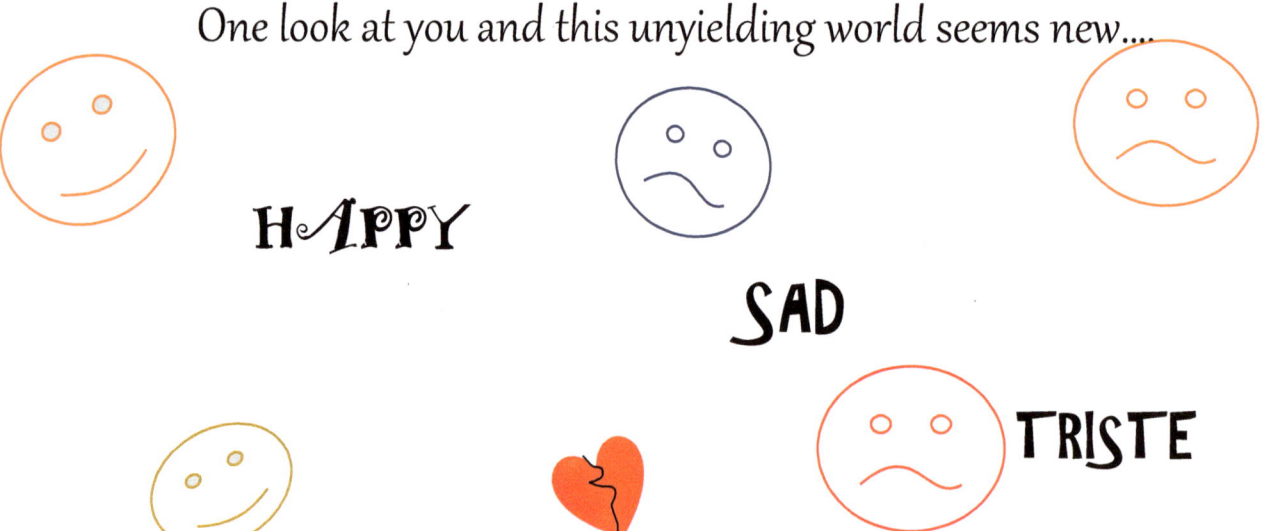

•Tell The World It's A Girl•

•#TELL THE WORLD IT'S A GIRL•

#BRAVE LEADER GIRL

#USE YOUR TIME WISELY

•#TELL THE WORLD IT'S A GIRL•

●Tell The World It's A Girl●

It's a Girl, a Royal little Girl; what an Angel you are! Whether near or far, from A to Z, you will always be mommy and daddy's brightest star.... Eyes twinkle brighter than the constellations and a smile as lovely as a full moon; we get lost in your radiance like a Sunday Afternoon....

●Tell The World It's A Girl●

Tell The World It's A Girl

It's a Girl, a Clever little Girl; what an Angel you are!

Bright eyes and picturesque smile, you're going places for sure;

Already displaying instant wit and guile....

You can be a genius in anything you choose.

Math, science, language, history, fashion, business, or art;

It doesn't matter as long as you have passion and heart!

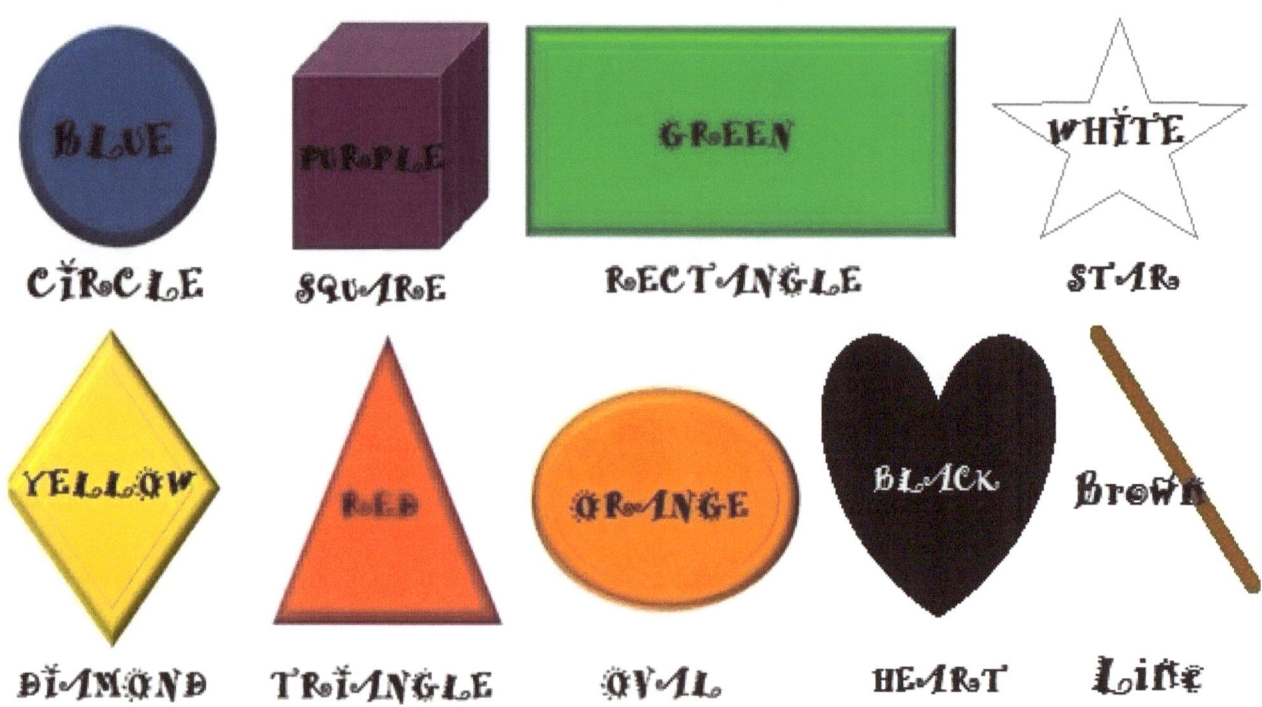

● Tell The World It's A Girl ●

The world is painted with shapes... Shape your world or someone else will!
#ICHOOSE

Tell The World It's A Girl

It's a Girl, an Impressionable little Girl;

What an Angel you are! Mommy and daddy's pint-sized reflection, good role models are what we vow to be, as your little eyes look up to thee....

So pure and full of possibility, we're so blessed and grateful to have this opportunity; the chance to help you grow with love, life, hope, and liberty....

●Tell The World It's A Girl●

●Tell The World It's A Girl●

It's a Girl, a Flowering little Girl; what an Angel you are!

Small hands, small feet... Oh my, how time flies, you have two front teeth....

Just yesterday we were carrying you along and today you're walking,

running, and eating all on your own. Please don't grow up too fast, be a

child as long as you can, and we'll promise to hold your precious hand.

When it's time, not a minute or moment before;

You'll be able to hold your own for sure....

●Tell The World It's A Girl●

It's a Girl, a **Loveable** little Girl; what an Angel you are!

So honey sweet, scrumptious and divine; God's best Heavenly surprise....

We are so honored to call you our daughter. Life has truly just begun.

From the rising of the Sun to the glorious Moon,

The Stars are singing a Heavenly tune;

Oh What A Blessing You Are....

It's a Girl,
A Future Leader little Girl; what an Angel you are!
Stand straight and tall our leading young daughter,
you were born with purpose and power....
Always do your best and accept nothing less.
Never dim your light to please others; you are better off being alone than amongst those who don't want the best for you. Use your mind and you can conquer anything. Your legs are sturdy and your heart is strong; your discerning spirit will help carry you along. Remember, you Lead by walking in your own truth. Utilize your heart for more than just beating; be passionate, wise, and prayerful.
Daughter, if you are authentically being yourself,
there is nothing you cannot do;
add a smile and there is
No way can you lose!

●Tell The World It's A Girl●

MY MIND & TONGUE ARE MY MOST POWERFUL INSTRUMENTS ... I WILL USE THEM BOTH WISELY

1) STOP THINKING "I WISH"
2) START SAYING "I WILL"
3) NOW PROVE YOURSELF RIGHT BY DOING IT!

●Tell The World It's A Girl●

Be Brave, Bold, and Brilliant! Go on adventures inside and out of your mind, reach for the stars and shine, shine, shine. Be Unapologetically You! Play outside; walk on skyscrapers, rumble with fire flies, make mud pies, & color outside the lines <This is your life> You only get one! So have fun, try lots of scary new things, and scour high in the trees; let your enchanting locs dance in the breeze. Read new books, discover exciting things to cook up, Waltz with hope, and write your own storybook. Dance pirouettes in the clouds, sing amongst the birds, and live, live, live. Ambitiously Pursue 10,000 pound dreams and hunt camouflaged "no's" until you reach your rainbow... Even if no one else believe,

Trust in Yourself & follow your heart; don't be afraid to capture your dreams because just like you, they are Beautiful***

●Tell The World It's A Girl●

10,000 LBS — DREAMS — 10,000 LBS

Reach for the highest apple and not the easiest

Hold onto your POWER young lady… GIRLS RULE!!

I AM prepared to get to
YES
1 NO 2 NO 3 NO
4 NO 5 NO 6 NO 7 NO 8 NO
9 NO
10 YES

I will patiently pursue my "Yes" with a loyal & optimistic attitude… I AM WORTH IT!

I WILL FIND A WAY OR MAKE ONE

Trust in yourself* & follow your heart; don't be afraid to capture your dreams* because just like you, they are Beautiful*

●Tell The World It's A Girl●

It's a Girl, a **Beautiful**, **Mesmerizing**, **Heaven-Sent**, **Spirited**, **Delightful**, **Royal**, **Clever**, Impressionable, **Flowering**, **Loveable**, and a **Future Leader** little Girl. An Extraordinary Daughter and a Ravishing Magnificence you are! So promising and full of life; a true treasure sent to Earth. We are happily in love with you! We'll shout it out from mountains high to valleys low, tell the whole world; so this day everyone will know about our greatest blessing named____! Say your name with us, ____, it's a magical sound. Go on, speak it proudly! Make your name sing over the lands. Yes You Can, Yes You Can, and Yes You Will! So, my dearest little Princess, when you feel small in this big-big world just listen for the birds singing, see fish swimming, the flowers blooming, and the animals dancing; They are all telling the world....

● Tell The World It's A Girl ●

It's our Beautiful little Girl, mommy and daddy's true life Angel, and

We are Happily in Love with YOU

●Tell The World It's A Girl●

About the Author

Jeanmela Murray was born and raised in Akron, Ohio. She is a graduate of American InterContinental University with a B.F.A in Fashion Merchandising and Fashion Design and later polished the city as a nail technician. Currently, Jeanmela resides in Atlanta, Georgia since 1999. In 2012 she became the mother of a beautiful little girl named Zoee, whom became the inspiration behind her wanting to write children's stories. What started out as a heart-felt message to her daughter, grew another love for wanting other children to feel the same type of love she saw in her daughter's eyes. Jeanmela wanted children to know they are beautiful and are God's gifts to the world. Zoee loves books and Jeanmela would love for other children to have that same excitement. She is in the process of developing a reading program called C.A.R.E (Children Are Reading Everyday) hoping to bring families together, morning, noon, and night. Through C.A.R.E, Jeanmela will allot her books to disadvantage families too facilitate stronger family bonds while they are going through tough times. She also would like other local authors to donate books to this cause. All parents deserve to see their children's face light up! I want to help families escape their challenging reality, even if only for a brief moment, says Jeanmela. She is optimistic her books will make a difference, getting families to read collectively and find comfort in the little things!

Additional Tidbits:

Jeanmela loves writing, music, photography, poetry, sports, designing jewelry, and nail polish! A few of her most favorite moments are the birth of her baby girl, seeing her daughter smile & giggle while running through the water sprinklers, and waking up to her kisses. Other notable highlights for Jeanmela are designing jewelry for Singer/Song writer India.Arie and Laurnea Wilkerson, autographing books for her first poetry book release, and watching her favorite athlete, Serena Williams play tennis.

In the future, Jeanmela will continue spreading love and encourage children to become their most powerful selves through her literary works for children.

Also Available from Author Jeanmela Murray:

● Tell The World It's A Boy ●

● Tell The World It's A Girl ●

www.ingramcontent.com/pod-product-compliance
Lightning Source LLC
Chambersburg PA
CBHW060823090426
42738CB00002B/93